S0-BAO-593

APR 2004

LEXINGTON PUBLIC LIBRARY

LEXINGTON, KENTUCKY

TATES CREEK BRANCH

DO NOT REMOVE CARD FROM POCKET

DEMCO

For Joanie, who loves poetry   —J.M.

The portrait of Lord Tennyson on page 4 by courtesy of
the National Portrait Gallery, London

Library of Congress Cataloging-in-Publication Data Available

Published by Sterling Publishing Company, Inc.
387 Park Avenue South, New York, N.Y. 10016
Text © 2003 by John Maynard
Illustrations © 2003 by Allen Garns
Distributed in Canada by Sterling Publishing
c/o Canadian Manda Group, One Atlantic Avenue, Suite 105
Toronto, Ontario, Canada M6K 3E7
Distributed in Great Britain and Europe by Chris Lloyd at Orca Book
Services, Stanley House, Fleets Lane, Poole BH15 3AJ, England
Distributed in Australia by Capricorn Link (Australia) Pty. Ltd.
P.O. Box 704, Windsor, NSW 2756, Australia

Printed in China
All rights reserved

Sterling ISBN 0-8069-6612-2

CONTENTS

INTRODUCTION

Tennyson is a poet whose personal life is closely connected to his work. He wrote from the heart, so to know his poems is to come close to his own hopes and fears, joys and losses. He lived a long time—from 1809 to 1892—practically through the entire nineteenth century. But his concerns—the beauty of the world, love of his friends and family, the sadness of loss—remain quite constant through those years.

He was deeply interested in the past and future of the British Isles, especially England itself, and in the myths and stories of ancient Greece and Rome. He could fire up descriptions so that they empower and haunt our minds—even when just a boy and young teenager. He would work up his words into vivid life while walking about country lanes near his home. When he had become a big-bearded grandfather poet of his country, he still could let out all the stops and sweep us away in his gorgeous, amazing descriptions, particularly of natural scenes.

Who was this boy and man who would become one of the famous poets of the English language—this poet whom we still read with interest and delight more than 100 years after his death?

Tennyson was quite a big success—because of his abilities as a poet—which is pretty unusual. He became well-to-do and had big houses, one almost like a castle. His marriage was pretty happy, and he had two children he got on with well. Everyone knew him as England's favorite poet—Poet Laureate, an honorary position conferred by the Queen on the best poet in the country. Finally, made a baron, Alfred Lord Tennyson became a new member of England's old nobility.

But let's look back before all this, before he became a household name and a major public man. Alfred was all his life shy and private—not much liking being a famous person, though glad that his poetry—and through him poetry in general—received so much recognition. He would rather we met him as a boy—young Alfred rather than Lord Tennyson—and get to know first the happy and the sad conditions from which his life and work developed.

The hard part of his life had mainly to do with what we would now call mental and emotional problems. In his family, as in so many families, there was the problem of a parent who drank, in Alfred's case, his father, George Tennyson. He also used abusive language and sometimes caused physical damage to the house or, very occasionally, to his children. The family feared he might go mad. Today help is available for such people, which makes it easier for their families, but in Alfred's time—he was born in 1809 (on August 5)—there wasn't much knowledge of what to do for such illnesses.

Alfred's grandfather was quite well-to-do, but ambitious and crude. Intent on his family becoming a very powerful one in England, he withdrew his financial and emotional support from Alfred's father and gave it to his uncle, a younger brother. The younger brother became a haughty man who tried to live like a great lord, castle and all. This undoubtedly added to the problems of George Tennyson, who felt betrayed and quarreled with his father all his life.

So Alfred grew up in a rather upset home, and often showed intense emotions in his songs or poems, though usually in the voice of someone else. Eventually he would make a great strength of the weakness and turbulence of his family, whereas, when a boy, he often was deeply hurt. That was the bad news of his life. The good news was all around him. He grew up in a really pretty and charming country village of England's Lincolnshire, where his father was the Church of England minister. Alfred loved the beautiful rolling hills, the animals, and the nearby seaside. Many of his best poems deal with landscapes in a world like his own or imaginary beautiful worlds.

His father, despite his problems, loved reading and poetry, especially the Latin and Greek poems that Alfred studied so carefully and learned so much from. His mother was a warm lover of English poetry and used to read it aloud to him. And many brothers and sisters made up a large caring family: there were eleven surviving children, of which Alfred was the third oldest. They also loved poetry—most of them—and shared their work with him. The younger ones asked him to be the family storyteller. Until Alfred's father died there was also a large comfortable home and good country neighbors to visit and talk with. Finally, Alfred had a good education, though he didn't like his first school where children were still whipped for misbehavior or bad work.

But his intelligent father trained him for Cambridge University, one of England's two great old universities; there he met and shared ideas about society, science, religion, and poetry with some of the brightest and most interesting university students of his time.

Alfred had started writing poetry by at least age 6. His first book of poetry was published with two of his brothers when he was 18. By the time he went to Cambridge, he was pretty much identified as a poet. Even his father, who had made his life so difficult, said he expected Alfred to be a great poet (perhaps seeing it as a way his son might be as successful as his brother's family). That didn't seem very likely, but at least Alfred felt recognized by his friends and family—all lovers of good poetry and of Alfred's quiet sense of humor. They also liked his ability to create poems in the voices of different characters, which he did in some of his best poems, such as "Ulysses" and

"Tithon" (pages 20 and 22). While still at Cambridge, Alfred published a serious book of shorter poems, this time under his name alone, and received some good reviews.

Then his troubles began again. The worst thing was that his best friend at Cambridge, Arthur Hallam, a fine, very intelligent man who was likely to have become a major figure in government—probably Prime Minister—died suddenly while on a trip to Vienna, Austria. Alfred took it like a blow and the blow was harder because Hallam had planned to marry Alfred's sister, Emily. Hallam was like family, as well as a best friend. Alfred would say that Hallam was even dearer to him than his brothers. The sad event seemed to bring up all the emotional upset of his boyhood. Alfred spent years grieving over his friend.

When the death of his father left his family with less and less money, Alfred seemed to pick up some of his father's feeling of resentment. He certainly had repeated bouts of depression. We now have good remedies for this illness, but at that time all doctors could offer was a series of cold baths in a so-called water cure. Alfred felt this treatment helped. But the best help in his distress seemed to be poetry. Fortunately for us, strong feelings often released his best use of language.

Within a year or so of Hallam's death, Alfred wrote some of his most powerful poems—"Ulysses," "Tithon," and "Break, Break, Break" (pages 20, 22, and 23). He kept writing about his loss for years and years,. Eventually, there emerged a major group of poems in memory of Hallam—*In Memoriam*, which means "in memory." His finest work, it is a full book of over 3,000 lines. Alfred worked on these poems and songs (or lyrics as they are also called) for 18 years, strengthening and reworking what he wrote. He organized them into a story about Hallam's death, his own grief, and the slow, slow process of his recovery from that grief. He used these poems to think through world problems he had discussed with Hallam that seemed increasingly urgent. Did geological discoveries—suggesting that the world was very old and filled with remains of extinct species (what we know as dinosaurs)—undercut religious faith? Was there a God who would bring him together someday with Hallam? Were we building, as Hallam hoped to build, a better society with a better life for all, in which we may develop our humanness further than ever before? Arthur Hallam and King Arthur, who tried to civilize early England, perhaps began to merge in his mind.

Meanwhile, as Alfred worked on this great set of poems, he lived a disconnected, unsettled life. He had had a love relation with his friend Emily Sellwood, but now gave that up. He seemed hardly part of the life around him. His next set of poems was heavily criticized. They seemed to some people too indulgent, too separated from everyday life. We now find some of them among his very best. To add to these problems, he lost his little inheritance in a wild speculation in a new manufacturing process.

Poetry, which allowed him to express his powerful feelings so well, again got him out of his troubles. In 1842, after about ten years' silence, he published some poems that were warmly applauded. Then in 1850 he finally issued *In Memoriam*. The poems were so good, and the issues they raised so meaningful, that they became suddenly tremendously popular. Queen Victoria and her husband Prince Albert loved them and chose Alfred to succeed Wordsworth as poet laureate. You can see several selections from this long, splendid poem of poems on pages 29–35.

In the same year that the poem was published, Alfred finally married Emily; they would have two sons, Hallam and Lionel, whom they brought up in their comfortable home. Emily and Alfred lived together until his death in 1892, although she had serious health problems in her last twenty years of life.

Alfred had made his peace with his loss and his own despair and began to speak publicly to his country. But we find, especially in *Maud*, that Alfred could still let a disturbed, angry young man speak. In the poem the speaker loses his love (the Maud of the title) and goes off to serve his country in the Crimean War (England against Russia). Alfred also wrote a poem addressed to his country, blaming the people who organized a military maneuver that took the lives of many soldiers ("The Charge of the Light Brigade," see page 36).

He then set about an enormous poetry project, the story of King Arthur, eventually called *Idylls of the King*. It was made up of a number of long poems, especially a set of stories—IDYLLS—in verse from tales of the mythical King Arthur. He had begun the story back in his years of loneliness, by writing about the death of Arthur. The poem thinks hard about the good and bad parts of England's position as the superpower of the nineteenth century. It deals with the moral issues of civilization at a time when England was developing the greatest empire ever seen. As they tell the tales of Arthur's knights conquering wild people and animals to create a just kingdom, they wonder how people need to behave in their personal lives to support the process of civilization. They don't talk about the issues of race and domination of others that we are concerned with today whenever one group tries to impose its values on another. Alfred's greatest emotional energies seem to have gone into his feelings about Arthur's death (see pages 44–45). Even in this long poem of idylls from the Round Table, we are treated, as in the return of the sword Excalibur, to sudden, illuminating, resonating descriptions.

All his life Alfred was supremely sensitive to moments that seem to take us outside our ordinary experience into trance-like, possibly religious states. He felt himself torn between his sense of everyday reality and moments of mystical insight. His last poem, "Crossing the Bar" (page 46), comes back to the powerful language of heading out to sea, as King Arthur did—not to Avalon, Arthur's mythical retreat, but rather to meet his Maker.

Tennyson is a master of description and the sound effects of poetry, and, like many other great poets, he speaks to us from his doubts, personal pain, and hard-earned understanding of himself and his world. I hope you enjoy reading his poems as much as I do!

THE MERMAID

The speaker dreams of being a mermaid and celebrates her beauty, which would charm sea creatures as well as mermen. The mermen would be so struck by her loveliness that they would forget that they were immortal, and feel as vulnerable and awestruck as mere human beings.

I

Who would be
A mermaid fair,
Singing alone,
Combing her hair
Under the sea,
In a golden curl
With a comb of pearl,
On a throne?

II

I would be a mermaid fair;
I would sing to myself the whole of the day;
With a comb of pearl I would comb my hair;
And still as I combed I would sing and say,
'Who is it loves me? who loves not me?'
I would comb my hair till my ringlets would fall
    Low adown, low adown,
From under my starry sea-bud crown
    Low adown and around,
And I should look like a fountain of gold
    Springing alone
    With a shrill inner sound,
    Over the throne
    In the midst of the hall;
Till that great sea-snake under the sea
From his coilèd sleeps in the central deeps

8

Would slowly trail himself sevenfold
Round the hall where I sate, and look in at the gate
With his large calm eyes for the love of me.
And all the mermen under the sea
Would feel their immortality
Die in their hearts for the love of me.

sate—*sat*

SONG—THE OWL

Night comes, then the first glimmer of dawn; all have gone indoors. But the owl stays out. The stream is still, unspeaking; the rooster sings his simple tune and repeats his song underneath the grass thatch roof of the barn.

I

When cats run home and light is come,
   And dew is cold upon the ground,
And the far-off stream is dumb,
   And the whirring sail goes round,
   And the whirring sail goes round;
     Alone and warming his five wits,
     The white owl in the belfry sits.

II

When merry milkmaids click the latch,
   And rarely smells the new-mown hay,
And the cock hath sung beneath the thatch
   Twice or thrice his roundelay,
   Twice or thrice his roundelay;
     Alone and warming his five wits,
     The white owl in the belfry sits.

dumb—*unable to speak, silent*
sail—*windmill vanes, acting and
   looking like inland sails*
belfry—*the bell tower of the
   village church*
thatch—*traditional roof made
   of grass*
roundelay—*a short, simple song
   with a refrain or chorus that
   is meant to be repeated*

THE EAGLE

This poem is a fragment, never completed, but very clear in its vivid description.
The eagle drops from his high place to descend and perhaps to take his prey.

He clasps the crag with crooked hands;
Close to the sun in lonely lands,
Ringed with the azure world, he stands.

The wrinkled sea beneath him crawls;
He watches from his mountain walls,
And like a thunderbolt he falls.

crag—*rugged rock or steep cliff*
azure—*sky blue*

SONG—A SPIRIT HAUNTS THE YEAR'S LAST HOURS

Tennyson imagines a spirit that hovers over the end of summer—yet along with the poet the spirit also grieves over dying nature.

I

A spirit haunts the year's last hours
Dwelling amid these yellowing bowers:
    To himself he talks;
For at eventide, listening earnestly,
At his work you may hear him sob and sigh
    In the walks;
    Earthward he boweth the heavy stalks
Of the mouldering flowers:
  Heavily hangs the broad sunflower
    Over its grave i' the earth so chilly;
  Heavily hangs the hollyhock,
    Heavily hangs the tiger-lily.

II

The air is damp, and hushed, and close,
As a sick man's room when he taketh repose
    An hour before death;
My very heart faints and my whole soul grieves
At the moist rich smell of the rotting leaves,
    And the breath
    Of the fading edges of box beneath,
And the year's last rose.
  Heavily hangs the broad sunflower
    Over its grave i' the earth so chilly;
  Heavily hangs the hollyhock,
    Heavily hangs the tiger-lily.

yellowing bowers—*flowers or vines that seem*
    to make a hiding place; they are turned for fall
eventide—*evening time*
boweth—*unusual form of the word "bow"*
mouldering—*beginning to rot*
repose—*taking a long rest*
box—*bordering shrub*

THE KRAKEN

The monster kraken, mythical figure from
Norwegian folklore, lies at the bottom of the ocean,
asleep until the day of God's judgment of men
when, according to the myth, he will wake and
come to the surface.

Below the thunders of the upper deep;
Far, far beneath in the abysmal sea,
His ancient, dreamless, uninvaded sleep
The Kraken sleepeth: faintest sunlights flee
About his shadowy sides: above him swell
Huge sponges of millennial growth and
       height;
And far away into the sickly light,
From many a wondrous grot and secret cell
Unnumbered and enormous polypi
Winnow with giant arms the slumbering
       green.
There hath he lain for ages and will lie
Battening upon huge seaworms in his sleep
Until the latter fire shall heat the deep;
Then once by man and angels to be seen,
In roaring he shall rise and on the surface die.

abysmal—*very deep*
millennial—*over a thousand years*
grot—*grotto or cave*
polypi—*octopuses*
battening—*fattening*

from THE LADY OF SHALOTT

In the old English world of Camelot a fairy lady lives alone, giving all her attention to her artistic weaving and not heeding the fruitful world around her. Tennyson loved the stories of Arthur and the Round Table. This is the first part of the poem.

PART I

On either side the river lie
Long fields of barley and of rye,
That clothe the wold and meet the sky;
And through the field the road runs by
    To many-towered Camelot;
And up and down the people go,
Gazing where the lilies blow
Round an island there below,
    The island of Shalott.

Willows whiten, aspens quiver,
Little breezes dusk and shiver
Through the wave that runs for ever
By the island in the river
    Flowing down to Camelot.
Four gray walls, and four gray towers,
Overlook a space of flowers,
And the silent isle imbowers
    The Lady of Shalott.

By the margin, willow-veiled,
Slide the heavy barges trailed
By slow horses; and unhailed
The shallop flitteth silken-sailed
    Skimming down to Camelot:
But who hath seen her wave her hand?
Or at the casement seen her stand?
Or is she known in all the land,
    The Lady of Shalott?

wold—*rolling plain without trees*
imbowers—*makes a kind of nest*
shallop—*open sailboat*
casement—*set of windows*
reapers—*farm workers cutting the harvest*
bearded barley—*barley with hair-like stalks*
uplands—*higher ground*

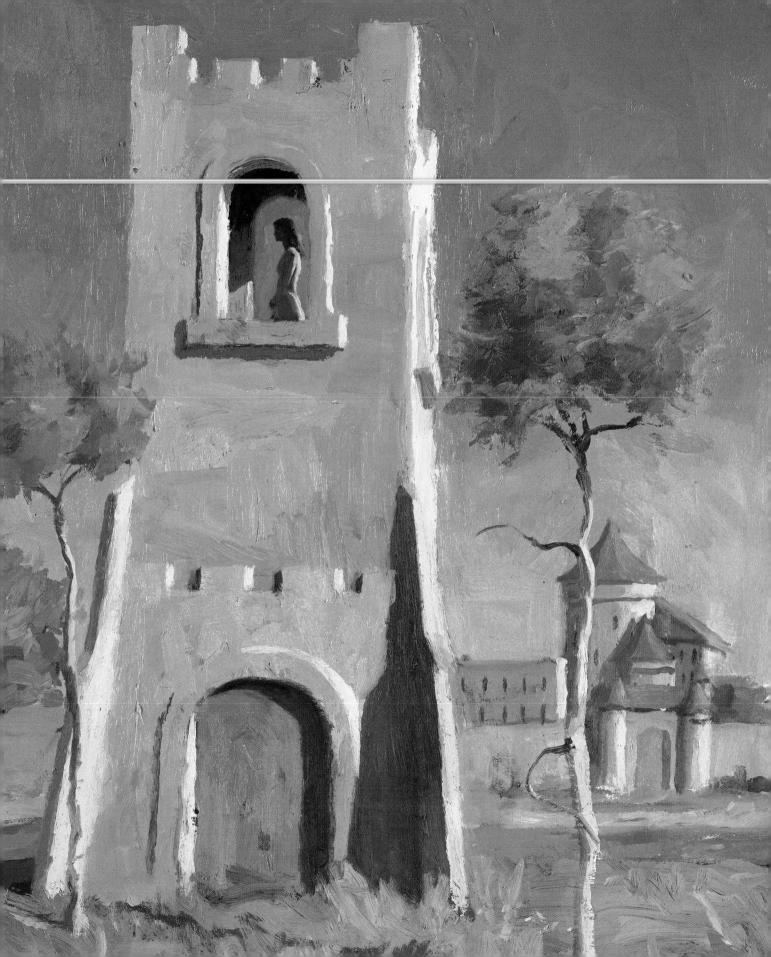

from THE HESPERIDES

The daughters of old Hesperus, with the help of a friendly dragon, guard the golden apples—though eventually they will be stolen away by Hercules. Tennyson seems to be identifying the golden apples of the Hesperides with the apple of Discord that the Trojan Paris gave to Venus, which brought about the legendary Trojan War. This is the last of four parts in this story from Greek myth.

Every flower and every fruit the redolent breath
Of this warm seawind ripeneth,
Arching the billow in his sleep;
But the landwind wandereth,
Broken by the highland-steep,
Two streams upon the violet deep:
For the western sun and the western star,
And the low west wind, breathing afar,
The end of day and beginning of night
Make the apple holy and bright;
Holy and bright, round and full, bright and blest,
Mellowed in a land of rest;
Watch it warily day and night;
All good things are in the west.
Till midnoon the cool east light
Is shut out by the round of the tall hillbrow;
But when the fullfaced sunset yellowly
Stays on the flowering arch of the bough,
The luscious fruitage clustereth mellowly,
Goldenkernelled, goldencored,
Sunset-ripened above on the tree.
The world is wasted with fire and sword,
But the apple of gold hangs over the sea.
Five links, a golden chain, are we,
Hesper, the dragon, and sisters three,
Daughters three,
Bound about
All round about
The gnarlèd bole of the charmèd tree.

redolent—*fragrant*
highland steep—*high slope*
bole—*tree trunk*

from THE LOTOS-EATERS

Ulysses, the hero of Homer's Odyssey, *and his men come in
their voyages to the wondrous land of the lotos, a plant that
offers forgetfulness to its eaters. The poem continues with
a song in which they celebrate the lotos fruit and the
mindlessness it gives them.*

'Courage!' he said, and pointed toward the land,
'This mounting wave will roll us shoreward soon.'
In the afternoon they came unto a land
In which it seemèd always afternoon.
All round the coast the languid air did swoon,
Breathing like one that hath a weary dream.
Full-faced above the valley stood the moon;
And like a downward smoke, the slender stream
Along the cliff to fall and pause and fall did seem.

A land of streams! some, like a downward smoke,
Slow-dropping veils of thinnest lawn, did go;
And some through wavering lights and shadows broke,
Rolling a slumbrous sheet of foam below.
They saw the gleaming river seaward flow
From the inner land: far off, three mountain-tops,
Three silent pinnacles of agèd snow,
Stood sunset-flushed: and, dewed with showery drops,
Up-clomb the shadowy pine above the woven copse.

The charmèd sunset lingered low adown
In the red West: through mountain clefts the dale
Was seen far inland, and the yellow down
Bordered with palm, and many a winding vale
And meadow, set with slender galingale;
A land where all things always seemed the same!
And round about the keel with faces pale,
Dark faces pale against that rosy flame,
The mild-eyed melancholy Lotos-eaters came.

from ULYSSES

Ulysses, home from his long travels after the battle of Troy, decides to set out to sea once more; this is his opening speech.

It little profits that an idle king,
By this still hearth, among these barren crags,
Matched with an agèd wife, I mete and dole
Unequal laws unto a savage race,
That hoard, and sleep, and feed, and know not me.

I cannot rest from travel: I will drink
Life to the lees: all times I have enjoyed
Greatly, have suffered greatly, both with those
That loved me, and alone; on shore, and when
Through scudding drifts the rainy Hyades
Vext the dim sea: I am become a name;
For always roaming with a hungry heart
Much have I seen and known; cities of men
And manners, climates, councils, governments,
Myself not least, but honoured of them all;
And drunk delight of battle with my peers,
Far on the ringing plains of windy Troy.
I am a part of all that I have met;
Yet all experience is an arch wherethrough
Gleams that untravelled world, whose margin fades
For ever and for ever when I move.
How dull it is to pause, to make an end,
To rust unburnished, not to shine in use!
As though to breathe were life. Life piled on life
Were all too little, and of one to me
Little remains: but every hour is saved
From that eternal silence, something more,
A bringer of new things; and vile it were
For some three suns to store and hoard myself,
And this gray spirit yearning in desire
To follow knowledge like a sinking star,
Beyond the utmost bound of human thought.
. . . .
Though much is taken, much abides; and though
We are not now that strength which in old days
Moved earth and heaven; that which we are, we are;
One equal temper of heroic hearts,
Made weak by time and fate, but strong in will
To strive, to seek, to find, and not to yield.

mete—*give out by measure*

dole—*give out in small portions*

lees—*sediment at bottom of the wine bottle, dregs*

scudding—*to run before a strong wind, in a boat*

Hyades—*five stars together in the constellation Taurus,
    indicating rain*

vext—*stirred up*

ringing plains—*ringing with battle sounds*

unburnished—*unpolished, by not being used*

One equal temper—*united in calm attitude*

from TITHON

Poor Tithon laments that he grows older and older. His wife is the goddess of the Dawn, ever young. His wife asked for immortality for him too so they could stay together, but forgot to ask Zeus that he stay young too. He will be turned into a grasshopper by the pitying gods, though this poem only prays for release. Tennyson wrote a later, longer version under the name "Tithonus."

Ay me! ay me! the woods decay and fall,
The vapours weep their substance to the ground,
Man comes and tills the earth and lies beneath,
And after many summers dies the rose.
Me only fatal immortality
Consumes: I wither slowly in thine arms,
Here at the quiet limit of the world,
A white-haired shadow roaming like a dream
The ever-silent spaces of the East,
Far-folded mists, and gleaming halls of morn.
    Ay me! ay me! what everlasting pain,
Being immortal with a mortal heart,
To live confronted with eternal youth:
To look on what is beautiful nor know
Enjoyment save through memory. Can thy love,
Thy beauty, make amends, though even now,
Close over us, the silver star, thy guide,
Shines in those tremulous eyes that fill with tears?

vapours—*mists*
rose—*in the later poem, "Tithonus," swan*
fatal immortality—*his bad fortune never
    to die but to become increasingly old*
tremulous—*trembling*

22

BREAK, BREAK, BREAK

Tennyson utters his immediate grief over his lost friend Arthur Hallam, the subject of his great poem, In Memoriam.

Break, break, break,
   On thy cold gray stones, O Sea!
And I would that my tongue could utter
   The thoughts that arise in me.

O well for the fisherman's boy,
   That he shouts with his sister at play!
O well for the sailor lad,
   That he sings in his boat on the bay!

And the stately ships go on
   To their haven under the hill;
But O for the touch of a vanished hand,
   And the sound of a voice that is still!

Break, break, break,
   At the foot of thy crags, O Sea!
But the tender grace of a day that is dead
   Will never come back to me.

OF OLD SAT FREEDOM ON THE HEIGHTS

The poet speaks of freedom as a woman who first kept her powerful knowledge apart from people, but then chose to bring it down from her heights to everyone who would take it. But the poet insists that with freedom must come love of truth and moderation that avoids extremes, qualities the woman also represents.

Of old sat Freedom on the heights,
  The thunders breaking at her feet:
Above her shook the starry lights:
  She heard the torrents meet.

There in her place she did rejoice,
  Self-gathered in her prophet-mind,
But fragments of her mighty voice
  Came rolling on the wind.

Then stept she down through town and field
  To mingle with the human race,
And part by part to men revealed
  The fulness of her face—

Grave mother of majestic works,
  From her isle-altar gazing down,
Who, God-like, grasps the triple forks,
  And, King-like, wears the crown:

Her open eyes desire the truth.
  The wisdom of a thousand years
Is in them. May perpetual youth
Keep dry their light from tears;

That her fair form may stand and shine,
  Make bright our days and light our dreams,
Turning to scorn with lips divine
  The falsehood of extremes!

SONG from *THE PRINCESS*: THE SPLENDOUR FALLS

In this long poem about a woman's college (an unheard of idea at that time), a group of friends enjoy a song of end of day outside, marked by the bugle's call.

The splendour falls on castle walls
    And snowy summits old in story:
The long light shakes across the lakes,
    And the wild cataract leaps in glory.
Blow, bugle, blow, set the wild echoes flying,
Blow, bugle; answer, echoes, dying, dying, dying.

O hark, O hear! how thin and clear,
    And thinner, clearer, farther going!
O sweet and far from cliff and scar
    The horns of Elfland faintly blowing!
Blow, let us hear the purple glens replying:
Blow, bugle; answer, echoes, dying, dying, dying.

O love, they die in yon rich sky,
    They faint on hill or field or river:
Our echoes roll from soul to soul,
    And grow for ever and for ever.
Blow, bugle, blow, set the wild echoes flying,
And answer, echoes, answer, dying, dying, dying.

cataract—*waterfall*
Elfland—*land of fairies*

SONG from *THE PRINCESS*: SWEET AND LOW

The princess sings this evening song, a lullaby that was set to music in 1863 by British composer Joseph Barnby and today it is one of the most popular of all lullabies.

Sweet and low, sweet and low,
    Wind of the western sea,
Low, low, breathe and blow,
    Wind of the western sea!
Over the rolling waters go,
Come from the dying moon, and blow,
    Blow him again to me;
While my little one, while my pretty one,
      sleeps.

Sleep and rest, sleep and rest,
    Father will come to thee soon;
Rest, rest, on mother's breast,
    Father will come to thee soon;
Father will come to his babe in the nest,
Silver sails all out of the west
    Under the silver moon:
Sleep, my little one, sleep, my pretty one,
      sleep.

SONG from *THE PRINCESS*: TEARS, IDLE TEARS

The princess sings a song filled with regret for days that have passed.

'Tears, idle tears, I know not what they mean,
Tears from the depth of some divine despair
Rise in the heart, and gather to the eyes,
In looking on the happy Autumn-fields,
And thinking of the days that are no more.

'Fresh as the first beam glittering on a sail,
That brings our friends up from the underworld,
Sad as the last which reddens over one
That sinks with all we love below the verge;
So sad, so fresh, the days that are no more.

'Ah, sad and strange as in dark summer dawns
The earliest pipe of half-awakened birds
To dying ears, when unto dying eyes
The casement slowly grows a glimmering square;
So sad, so strange, the days that are no more.

'Dear as remembered kisses after death,
And sweet as those by hopeless fancy feigned
On lips that are for others; deep as love,
Deep as first love, and wild with all regret;
O Death in Life, the days that are no more.'

verge—*horizon*
casement—*set of windows*
feigned—*pretended*

IN MEMORIAM: V

The title means "in memory." Tennyson's best friend Arthur Hallam died when he and Tennyson were still young men. Tennyson wrote his greatest work grieving and honoring his friend in a long series of short poems. In this one he justifies writing so much on his loss.

I sometimes hold it half a sin
   To put in words the grief I feel;
   For words, like Nature, half reveal
And half conceal the Soul within.

But, for the unquiet heart and brain,
   A use in measured language lies;
   The sad mechanic exercise,
Like dull narcotics, numbing pain.

In words, like weeds, I'll wrap me o'er,
   Like coarsest clothes against the cold;
   But that large grief which these enfold
Is given in outline and no more.

weeds—*clothes, often for mourning*

IN MEMORIAM: XI

A calm beautiful day; but the poet can't help thinking of his lost friend, who in death is only too calm.

Calm is the morn without a sound,
   Calm as to suit a calmer grief,
   And only through the faded leaf
The chestnut pattering to the ground:

Calm and deep peace on this high wold,
   And on these dews that drench the furze,
   And all the silvery gossamers
That twinkle into green and gold:

Calm and still light on yon great plain
   That sweeps with all its autumn bowers,
   And crowded farms and lessening towers,
To mingle with the bounding main:

Calm and deep peace in this wide air,
   These leaves that redden to the fall;
   And in my heart, if calm at all,
If any calm, a calm despair:

Calm on the seas, and silver sleep,
   And waves that sway themselves in rest,
   And dead calm in that noble breast
Which heaves but with the heaving deep.

wold—*open field*
furze—*spiny shrub*
gossamers—*fine cobwebs*
bowers—*enclosed places*

In Memoriam: XXVII

The poet would not want to live without feelings, even though it has been so painful for him to lose his friend. The ending has become very well known.

I envy not in any moods
    The captive void of noble rage,
    The linnet born within the cage,
That never knew the summer woods:

I envy not the beast that takes
    His license in the field of time,
    Unfettered by the sense of crime,
To whom a conscience never wakes;

Nor, what may count itself as blest,
    The heart that never plighted troth
    But stagnates in the weeds of sloth;
Nor any want-begotten rest.

I hold it true, whate'er befall;
    I feel it, when I sorrow most;
    'Tis better to have loved and lost
Than never to have loved at all.

linnet—*small, brown songbird*
license—*doing whatever he wants*
unfettered—*not restrained*
plighted troth—*promised marriage*
weeds—*clothes*
sloth—*laziness*
want-begotten—*coming from need only*
befall—*happen*

IN MEMORIAM: LIV

The poet trusts that God orders and makes
meaningful even bad things—but who is he, a
mere baby before God, to know this?

Oh, yet we trust that somehow good
   Will be the final goal of ill,
   To pangs of nature, sins of will,
Defects of doubt, and taints of blood;

That nothing walks with aimless feet;
   That not one life shall be destroyed,
   Or cast as rubbish to the void,
When God hath made the pile complete;

That not a worm is cloven in vain;
   That not a moth with vain desire
   Is shrivelled in a fruitless fire,
Or but subserves another's gain.

Behold, we know not anything;
   I can but trust that good shall fall
   At last—far off—at last, to all,
And every winter change to spring.

So runs my dream: but what am I?
   An infant crying in the night:
   An infant crying for the light:
And with no language but a cry.

taints—*genetic/emotional problems*
pile—*creation*
cloven—*cut in half*
subserves—*to serve another*

IN MEMORIAM: *from* CVI

The poet celebrates the New Year and looks to an end of his grieving over his friend and to better times for all.

Ring out, wild bells, to the wild sky,
　The flying cloud, the frosty light:
　The year is dying in the night;
Ring out wild bells, and let him die.

Ring out the old, ring in the new,
　Ring, happy bells, across the snow:
　The year is going, let him go;
Ring out the false, ring in the true.

Ring out the grief that saps the mind,
　For those that here we see no more;
　Ring out the feud of rich and poor,
Ring in redress to all mankind.

Ring out a slowly dying cause,
　And ancient forms of party strife;
　Ring in the nobler modes of life,
With sweeter manners, purer laws.

Ring out the want, the care, the sin,
　The faithless coldness of the times;
　Ring out, ring out my mournful rhymes,
But ring the fuller minstrel in.

Ring out false pride in place and blood,
　The civic slander and the spite;
　Ring in the love of truth and right,
Ring in the common love of good.

Ring out old shapes of foul disease;
　Ring out the narrowing lust of gold;
　Ring out the thousand wars of old,
Ring in the thousand years of peace.

redress—*make right*

IN MEMORIAM: CXXI

Hesper, the evening star, Phosphor, the morning star, are really the same thing, though one stands for sleep and rest, the other for waking and activity. We know the star as the planet Venus.

Sad Hesper o'er the buried sun
   And ready, thou, to die with him,
   Thou watchest all things ever dim
And dimmer, and a glory done:

The team is loosen'd from the wain,
   The boat is drawn upon the shore;
   Thou listenest to the closing door,
And life is darken'd in the brain.

Bright Phosphor, fresher for the night,
   By thee the world's great work is heard
   Beginning, and the wakeful bird;
Behind thee comes the greater light:

The market boat is on the stream,
   And voices hail it from the brink;
   Thou hear'st the village hammer clink,
And see'st the moving of the team.

Sweet Hesper-Phosphor, double name
   For what is one, the first, the last,
   Thou, like my present and my past,
Thy place is changed; thou art the same.

wain—*horsecart*

In Memoriam: CXXVI

The poet ends his great poem of grief, professing his faith in God, which is the same thing as Love. He ends with a deep knowing that all is well despite the appearance of loss on earth.

Love is and was my Lord and King,
    And in his presence I attend
    To hear the tidings of my friend,
Which every hour his couriers bring.

Love is and was my King and Lord,
    And will be, though as yet I keep
    Within his court on earth, and sleep
Encompass'd by his faithful guard,

And hear at times a sentinel
    Who moves about from place to place,
    And whispers to the worlds of space,
In the deep night, that all is well.

tidings—*news*
couriers—*messengers*
sentinel—*watchman*

35

from THE CHARGE OF THE LIGHT BRIGADE

The poet responded to news reports of very heavy and unnecessary losses in a cavalry charge in the Crimean War (1854), fought by England against Russia. This poem was meant to be read aloud, and it repeats some strong statements it wants to bring home to the listener. Note also repeated words in different lines. Here is the first half of the poem.

I

Half a league, half a league,
   Half a league onward,
All in the valley of Death
   Rode the six hundred.
'Forward, the Light Brigade!
Charge for the guns!' he said:
   Into the valley of Death
   Rode the six hundred.

II

'Forward, the Light Brigade!'
Was there a man dismayed?
Not though the soldier knew
   Some one had blundered:
Their's not to make reply,
Their's not to reason why,
Their's but to do and die:
Into the valley of Death
   Rode the six hundred.

III

Cannon to right of them,
Cannon to left of them,
Cannon in front of them
   Volleyed and thundered;
Stormed at with shot and shell,
Boldly they rode and well,
Into the jaws of Death,
Into the mouth of Hell
   Rode the six hundred.

league——*three miles*

37

THE FLOWER

Have you ever felt that someone stole one of your ideas? Tennyson did. First his work was new, too new. Then others stole it and it appeared everywhere. Now people are saying that it is nothing special.

Once in a golden hour
    I cast to earth a seed.
Up there came a flower,
    The people said, a weed.

To and fro they went
    Through my garden-bower,
And muttering discontent
    Cursed me and my flower.

Then it grew so tall
    It wore a crown of light,
But thieves from o'er the wall
    Stole the seed by night.

Sowed it far and wide
    By every town and tower,
Till all the people cried
    'Splendid is the flower.'

Read my little fable:
    He that runs may read.
Most can raise the flowers now,
    For all have got the seed.

And some are pretty enough,
    And some are poor indeed;
And now again the people
    Call it but a weed.

FLOWER IN THE CRANNIED WALL

The poet finds the mystery of life in the wonder of a small flower flourishing
so well, even in the chinks of an old wall.

Flower in the crannied wall,
I pluck you out of the crannies,
I hold you here, root and all, in my hand,
Little flower—but *if* I could understand
What you are, root and all, and all in all,
I should know what God and man is.

crannies—*small opening, as in a rock wall*

from *MAUD*: SECTION XXII

This was Tennyson's favorite poem for reading aloud. It tells the story of a young man who loses his love, goes mad, and then joins the army. In these first verses, the young man calls his friend to join him in the garden and look at the planet Venus, which he calls the planet of Love because Venus is the goddess of love.

I

Come into the garden, Maud,
   For the black bat, night, has flown,
Come into the garden, Maud,
   I am here at the gate alone;
And the woodbine spices are wafted abroad,
   And the musk of the rose is blown.

II

For a breeze of morning moves,
   And the planet of Love is on high,
Beginning to faint in the light that she loves
   On a bed of daffodil sky,
To faint in the light of the sun she loves
   To faint in his light, and to die.

woodbine—*honeysuckle*

IN THE VALLEY OF THE CAUTERETZ

The poet visits a beautiful valley in the Pyrenees that makes
him strongly recall being there years before with his friend
Arthur Hallam.

All along the valley, stream that flashest white,
Deepening thy voice with the deepening of the night,
All along the valley, where thy waters flow,
I walked with one I loved two and thirty years ago.
All along the valley, while I walked today,
The two and thirty years were a mist that rolls away;
For all along the valley, down thy rocky bed,
Thy living voice to me was as the voice of the dead,
And all along the valley, by rock and cave and tree,
The voice of the dead was a living voice to me.

from *Idylls of the King*:
The Passing of Arthur

When Arthur came into his power, the Lady of the Lake mysteriously gave him his wonderful sword Excalibur. Now, knowing his end, King Arthur commands his knight to return the sword to the lake from which it came. This is from the end section of Tennyson's Idylls of the King, *though it was written much earlier than the rest of that long poem about Arthur and the Round Table.*

> Then quickly rose Sir Bedivere, and ran,
> And, leaping down the ridges, lightly, plunged
> Among the bulrush beds, and clutched the sword,
> And strongly wheeled and threw it. The great brand
> Made lightnings in the splendour of the moon,
> And flashing round and round, and whirled in an arch,
> Shot like a streamer of the northern morn,
> Seen where the moving isles of winter shock
> By night, with noises of the Northern Sea.
> So flashed and fell the brand Excalibur:
> But ere he dipt the surface, rose an arm
> Clothed in white samite, mystic, wonderful,
> And caught him by the hilt, and brandished him
> Three times, and drew him under in the mere.
> And lightly went the other to the King.
>
> Then spoke King Arthur, drawing thicker breath:
> 'Now see I by thine eyes that this is done.
> Speak out: what is it thou hast heard, or seen?'
>
> And answer made the bold Sir Bedivere:
> 'Sir King, I closed mine eyelids, lest the gems
> Should blind my purpose, for I never saw,
> Nor shall see, here or elsewhere, till I die,
> Not though I live three lives of mortal men,
> So great a miracle as yonder hilt.
> Then with both hands I flung him, wheeling him;
> But when I looked again, behold an arm,
> Clothed in white samite, mystic, wonderful,
> That caught him by the hilt, and brandished him
> Three times, and drew him under in the mere.'

Sir Bedivere—*Arthur's faithful knight and supporter*

bulrush beds—*plants of bulrush growing near the water, with tall stalks*

streamer of the Northern morn—*Northern lights in the sky, aurora borealis*

isles of winter—*icebergs*

samite—*heavy silk, often with gold and silver woven into it*

hilt—*handle of the sword*

brandished—*waved around as if in battle*

mere—*lake, where the sword came from originally*

43

from MORTE D'ARTHUR

Sir Bedivere laments Arthur's leaving, at his death, on a boat for Avalon, and the end of Camelot. But the King reassures him: new times will bring new order. This is from the earlier version, called "Morte d'Arthur," the death of Arthur. With changes, it became "The Passing of Arthur" in Idylls of the King.

Then loudly cried the bold Sir Bedivere:
'Ah! my Lord Arthur, whither shall I go?
Where shall I hide my forehead and my eyes?
For now I see the true old times are dead,
When every morning brought a noble chance,
And every chance brought out a noble knight.
Such times have been not since the light that led
The holy Elders with the gift of myrrh.
But now the whole ROUND TABLE is dissolved
Which was an image of the mighty world;
And I, the last, go forth companionless,
And the days darken round me, and the years,
Among new men, strange faces, other minds.'

And slowly answered Arthur from the barge:
'The old order changeth, yielding place to new,
And God fulfils Himself in many ways,
Lest one good custom should corrupt the world.

Avalon—*the mythical land to which Arthur was taken
at his end; the legend was that he would return someday*

CROSSING THE BAR

The poet, like his character Ulysses, thinks of life's end as heading out to sea; but hopes to meet
God after he has crossed the sandbar and moved into open ocean. Tennyson wanted all collections
of his poetry to end with this poem.

Sunset and evening star,
    And one clear call for me!
And may there be no moaning of the bar,
    When I put out to sea,

But such a tide as moving seems asleep,
    Too full for sound and foam,
When that which drew from out the boundless deep
    Turns again home.

Twilight and evening bell,
    And after that the dark!
And may there be no sadness of farewell,
    When I embark;

For though from out our bourne of Time and Place
    The flood may bear me far,
I hope to see my Pilot face to face
    When I have crost the bar.

bourne—*boundary, end*
pilot—*the sailor who steers a ship*
crost—*crossed*